M

costume in

National
Gallery

costume in

art

National
Gallery

Jean-Auguste-Dominique Ingres: detail of *Madame Moitessier*

First published in the United States in 1998 by
Watson-Guptill Publications, Inc.
a division of BPI Communications, Inc.
1515 Broadway
New York, NY 10036

Series Editor: Ljiljana Ortolja-Baird
Designer: Bet Ayer

Library of Congress Catalog Card Number: 98-85854

ISBN: 0-8230-0333-7

First published in the United Kingdom in 1998 by
MQ Publications Ltd.
254–258 Goswell Road
London EC1V 7EB

Printed and bound in Italy

1 2 3 4 5 6 7 8 / 05 04 03 02 01 00 99 98

Title page: Frederic, Baron Leighton of Stretton,
*Cimabue's Celebrated Madonna is carried in Procession through the
Streets of Florence,* The Royal Collection © 1998 Her Majesty
Queen Elizabeth II, on loan to the National Gallery

Anthony van Dyck: detail of *Lord John Stuart and his Brother, Lord Bernard Stuart*

6

INTRODUCTION

'As painting, so poetry'. Like all siblings, the Sister
Arts are rivals and allies. In the mirrors they hold up
to nature we see ourselves reflected from varying
angles and by different lights.

The National Gallery in London houses many of the
world's finest European pictures – and in one respect
they demonstrate painting's superiority to literature.
Poets can praise a satin gown, and satirists mock the
shirt collar's lofty pretensions – but only painters are
able to show what these garments looked like and how
they were once worn.

Costume in Art is not a history of dress, however,
the myriad of details taken from each painting provides
a wonderful overview of the sartorial concerns of past
ages. Wittily juxtaposing texts and images, it allows us
to eavesdrop on past conversations – the complaint of a
man to his tailor, a young girl's plea to her father for
a new bonnet – while simultaneously illustrating the
timeless significance of fashion. A lace ruff forever
distinguishes a queen from a dairy maid.

Erika Langmuir
Head of Education, National Gallery, 1988–1995

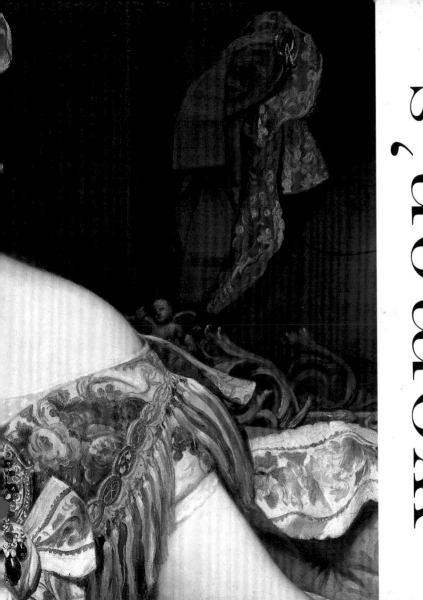

women's clothes

EGLON HENDRIK VAN DER NEER
(1634?–1703) Dutch
Judith
about 1678

Needle, needle, dip and dart,
Thrusting up and down,
Where's the man could ease a heart
Like a satin gown?

See the stitches curve and crawl
Round the cunning seams—
Patterns thin and sweet and small
As a lady's dreams.

Wantons go in bright brocade;
Brides in organdie;
Gingham's for the plighted maid;
Satin's for the free!

Wool's to line a miser's chest;
Crape's to calm the old;
Velvet hides an empty breast;
Satin's for the bold!

Lawn is for a bishop's yoke;
Linen's for a nun;
Satin is for wiser folk—
Would the dress were done!

Satin glows in candlelight—
Satin's for the proud!
They will say who watch at night,
'What a fine shroud!'

The Satin Dress,
DOROTHY PARKER, 1926

JEAN-SIMÉON CHARDIN (1699–1779) French
The Cistern (La Fontaine)
1733 or later

So, thought I, I had better get myself at once equipped in
the dress that will become my condition; and though it may
look poor to what I have been used to wear of late days, yet
it will serve me, when I am with you, for a good holiday and
Sunday suit, and what, by a blessing on my industry, I may,
perhaps, make shift to keep up to...

I bought of Farmer Nichols's wife and daughters, a good
sad-coloured stuff of their own spinning, enough to make me
a gown and two petticoats; and I made robings and faceings
of a pretty bit of printed callico I had by me.

I had a pretty good camblet quilted coat, that I
thought might do tolerably well; and I bought two flannel
under-coats; not so good as my swan-skin and fine linen
ones, but what will keep me warm ...

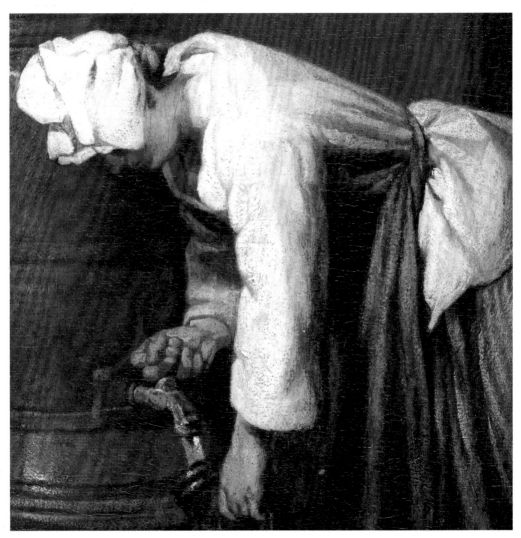

16

I got some pretty good Scots cloth, and made me, at mornings and nights, when nobody saw me, two shifts; and I have enough left for two shirts, and two shifts, for you, my dear father and mother. When I come home, I'll make 'em up, and desire your acceptance of them.

Then I bought of a pedlar, two pretty-enough round-eared caps, a little straw hat, and a pair of knit mittens turned up with white callico; and two pair of ordinary blue worsted hose, that make a smartish appearance, with white clocks, I'll assure you! and two yards of black riband for my shift-sleeves, and to serve as a necklace.

from *Pamela; or Virtue Rewarded*,
SAMUEL RICHARDSON, 1740–41

ANTHONY VAN DYCK (1599–1641) Flemish
Lady Elizabeth Thimbelby and Dorothy, Viscountess Andover
about 1637

The upstart impudence and innovation of naked breasts, and cutting and hallowing downe the neck of women's garments below their shoulders, an exorbitant and shamefull enormity and habit, much worn by our semi-Adamits, is another piece of refined Barbarisme…Another foolish affection there is in young Virgins, though grown big enough to be wiser, but that they are led blind-fold by custome to fashion pernitious beyond imagination; who thinking a Slender-Waste a great

beauty, strive all that they possibly can by streight-lacing themselves, to attain unto a wand-like smalnesse of Waste, never thinking themselves fine enough untill they can span their Waste.

from *The Artificial Changeling*,
JOHN BULWER, 1650

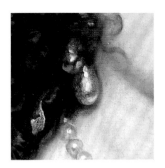

Elizabeth Louise Vigée Le Brun (1755–1842)
French
Self Portrait in a Straw Hat
after 1782

As I had a horror of the clothes women then wore, I made
every effort to make them a little more picturesque, and
I was delighted, when I had gained the confidence of my
models, to be able to drape them as my imagination
suggested. Shawls were not worn then: but I spread large
scarves, lightly folded around the body and over the arms,
with which I tried to imitate the beautiful manner of the
draperies of Raphael and Domenichino…I would not
tolerate the use of powder. I persuaded the beautiful
Duchesse de Gramont-Caderousse not to use any when she
was to be painted. This reminds me that in 1786 when I
painted the Queen [Marie Antoinette], I begged her not to
put on powder and to part her hair on her forehead. 'I shall
be the last to follow that fashion,' the Queen said laughingly;
'I do not want it said that I have thought of it in order to
hide my large forehead.'

I have tried as far as possible to give to the women I
painted their true attitude and facial expression. Those who
had none, I painted as languorous and nonchalant.

from *Souvenirs*,
Elizabeth Louise Vigée Le Brun, about 1835

25

PIERRE-AUGUSTE RENOIR
(1841–1919) French
The Umbrellas
about 1881–86

Skirts were more tiresome than
painful, but they could be very
tiresome indeed. By the time
I was eighteen, my skirts came
right down to the ground, and
Sunday dresses had to have little
trains behind. It was difficult to
walk freely in the heavy tweed
'walking skirts', which kept on
catching between the knees.

Round the bottom of these skirts I had, with my own hands, sewn two and a half yards of 'brush braid', to collect the worst of the mud; for they inevitably swept the roads, however carefully I might hold them up behind; and the roads were then much muddier than the tarred roads are now. Afterwards the crusted mud had to be brushed off, which might take an hour or more to do.

from *Period Piece,*
A Cambridge Childhood
GWEN RAVERAT, 1952

31

Johann Zoffany (1733?–1810) German
Mrs Oswald
probably about 1760–65

Most English women are fair and have pink and white
complexions, soft though expressive eyes, and slim,
pretty figures, of which they are very proud and take great
care, for in the morning, as soon as they rise they don a sort
of bodice which encircles their waists tightly. They are fond
of ornaments, and old and young alike, wear four or five
patches, and always two large ones on the forehead.
Few women curl their hair, and they seldom wear ribbons,
feathers, or flowers, but little head-dresses of cambric or of
magnificent lace on their pretty, well-kept hair. They pride
themselves on their neatly shod feet, on their fine linen, and
on their gowns, which are made according to the season
either of rich silk or of cotton from the Indies.

Very few women wear woollen gowns. Even servant-maids wear silks on Sundays and holidays, when they are almost as well dressed as their mistresses. Gowns have enormous hoops, short and very wide sleeves, and it is the fashion to wear little mantles of scarlet or of black velvet, and small hats of straw that are vastly becoming. Ladies even of the highest rank are thus attired when they go walking or to make a simple visit.

from *A Foreign View of England in the Reigns of George I & George II*, CÉSAR DE SAUSSURE, 1729

37

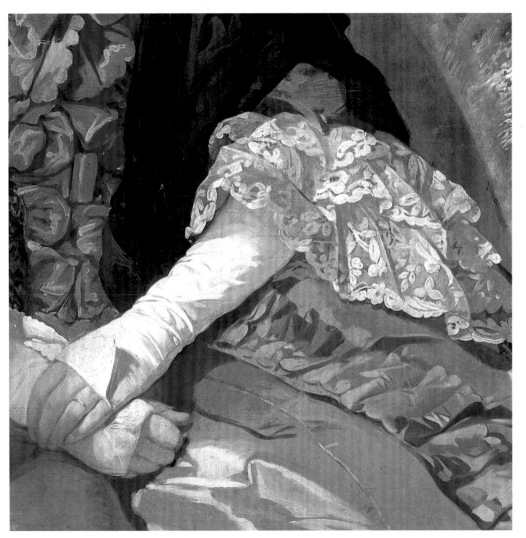

men's clothes

ANTHONY VAN DYCK (1599–1641) Flemish
Lord John Stuart and his Brother, Lord Bernard Stuart
about 1638

Fashion is an odd jumble of contradictions, of sympathies and antipathies. It exists only by its being participated among a number of persons, and the essence is destroyed by being communicated to a greater number. It is a continual struggle between the 'the great vulgar and the small' to get the start of, or keep up with each other in the race of appearances, by an adoption on the part of the one of such external and fantastic symbols as strike the attention and excite the envy or admiration of the beholder, and which are no sooner made known and exposed to public view for this purpose, than they are successfully copied by the multitude, the slavish herd of imitators, who do not wish to be behindhand with their betters in outward show and pretensions, and then sink, without any farther notice into disrepute and contempt.

44

Thus fashion lives only in a perpetual round of giddy imitation and restless vanity. To be old fashioned is the greatest crime a coat or a hat can be guilty of. To look like nobody else is a sufficiently mortifying reflection; to be in danger of being mistaken for one of the rabble is worse. Fashion constantly begins and ends in the two things it abhors most, singularity and vulgarity.

from 'On Fashion', *Sketches and Essays*,
WILLIAM HAZLITT, 1839

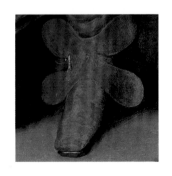

46

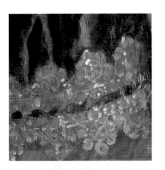

DOMENICO GHIRLANDAIO (1449–1494) Italian
A Legend of Saints Justus and Clement of Volterra
probably 1479

...a yong Squyer
A lovyere, and a lusty bacheler,
With lokkes crulle, as they were leyd in presse.
Of twenty yeer of age he was, I gesse.
Of his stature he was of evene lengthe,
And wonderly deliver, and greet of strengthe.
And he had been somtyme in chivachye,
In Flaundres, in Artoys, and Picardye,
And born him wel, as of so litel space,
In hope to stonden in his lady grace.
Embrouded was he, as it wore a mede
Al full of fresshe floures, whyte and rede.
Singinge he was, or floytinge, al the day;
He was as fresh as is the month of May.
Short was his goune, with sleves longe and wyde.

from *The Canterbury Tales*,
GEOFFREY CHAUCER, from 1387

50

51

52

53

GERARD TER BORCH (1617–1681) Dutch
Portrait of a Young Man
probably about 1663–64

Dress is a very foolish thing; and yet it is a very foolish thing
for a man not to be well dressed, according to his rank and
way of life; and it is so far from being a disparagement to
any man's understanding, that it is rather a proof of it, to be
as well dressed as those whom he lives with: the difference in
this case, between a man of sense and a fop, is, that a fop
values himself upon his dress; and the man of sense laughs
at it, at the same time that he knows that he must not
neglect it; there are a thousand foolish customs of this kind,
which, not being criminal, must be complied with, and even
cheerfully, by men of sense. Diogenes the Cynic was a wise
man for despising them, but a fool for showing it.

from *Letters to His Son*,
LORD CHESTERFIELD, published in 1745

56

WILLEM DUYSTER (1599–1635) Dutch
Soldiers Fighting over Booty in a Barn
about 1623–24

Take a creature that nature has form'd without any
brains…
And now for to dress up my beau with a grace,
Let a well frizzled wig be set off from his face;
With a bag quite in taste, from Paris just come,
That was made and tied up by Monsieur Frisson:
With powder quite grey, then his head is complete;
If dress'd in the fashion, no matter for wit;
With a pretty black beaver tuck'd under his arm,
If placed on his head, it might keep it too warm;
Then a black solitaire his neck to adorn,
Like those of Versailles by the courtiers there worn;

His hands must be cover'd with fine Brussels lace,
With a sparkling brilliant his finger to grace;
Next a coat of embroidery from foreigners come,
'Twou'd be quite unpolite to have one wrought at home;
With cobweb silk stockings his legs to befriend,
Two pair underneath, his lank calves to amend;
With breeches in winter would cause one to freeze,
To add to his height, must not cover his knees;
A pair of smart pumps made up of grain'd leather;
So thin he can't venture to tread on a feather;
His buckles like diamonds must glitter and shine
Should they cost fifty pounds they would not be too fine;

A repeater by Graham, which the hours reveals,
Almost over-balanc'd with knick-knacks and seals;
A mouchoir with musk his spirits to cheer,
Though he scents the whole room, that no soul can
      come near;
A gold-hilted sword with jewels inlaid,
So the scabbard's but cane, no matter for blade;
A word-knot of ribband to answer his dress,
Most completely tied up with tassels of lace;
Thus fully equipp'd and attir'd for show,
Observe, pray, ye belles, that fam'd thing call'd a beau.

from *Monsieur-à-la-mode*,
ANONYMOUS, 18th century

JEAN-AUGUSTE-DOMINIQUE
INGRES (1780–1867) French
Monsieur de Norvins
1811–12

'Pray, is the fashion for the shirt
collar to stand as high as the
corners of the eyes?'

from *The Early Married Life of Maria Josepha*,
LADY STANLEY, 1800

65

POMPEO GIROLAMO BATONI (1708–1787) Italian
Portrait of a Gentleman
probably 1760s

(Henry Purefoy to his tailor)
Do they button their Cloathes with Silver or Gold Buttons or
continue to wear laced waistcoats of silk or cloth?

The Gold laced waistcoat you made mee last year has done
you no credit in the making, it gapes so intolerably before
at the bottom, when I button it at ye waistbone of my
breeches and stand upright it gapes at the bottom beyond
my breeches and everybody takes notice of it. As to my size I
am partly the same bignesse as I was when in Town last, but
you made the last cloathes a little too straight.

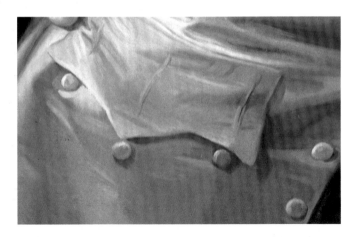

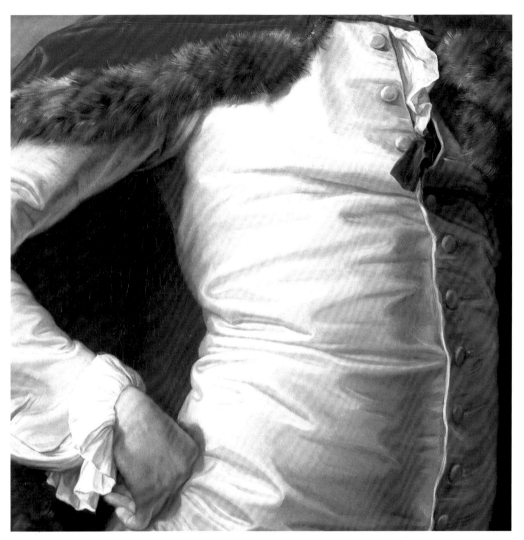

…the green waistcoat is a very poor silk…The sleeves of the coat come quite down to my wrist and are a great deall longer than ye coat you made mee last year…let mee know if they wear their coat sleeves longer than they did last year…

from *Purefoy Letters* 1735–53,
Henry Purefoy

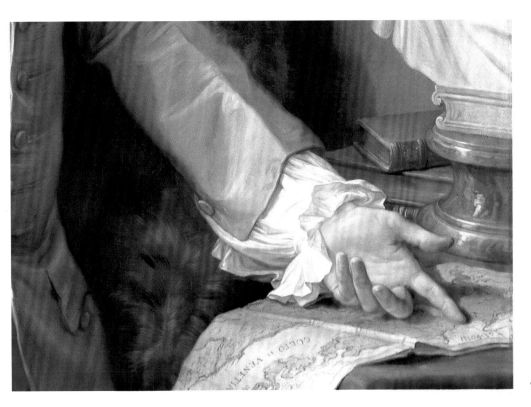

JUSTUS SUSTERMANS
(1597–1681) Flemish
*Double Portrait of the Grand
Duke Ferdinand II of Tuscany
and his Wife Vittoria della Rovere*
probably 1660s

'We know, Mr Weller – we who
are men of the world – that a
good uniform must work its way
with women, sooner or later.'

from *Pickwick Papers*,
CHARLES DICKENS, 1836–37

73

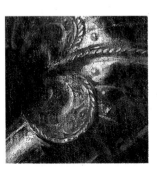

75

children's clothes

Jacob Maris (1837–1899) Dutch
A Girl Seated Outside a House
1867

…the reason is why I write because I want a few things, my Bonnet is so dirty I can scarcely for shame wear it. I wish you would send me another for if I get this cleaned I have no other to wear while it is cleaned and besides my new one would fit me all next summer for if I stop here I must have things it is getting quite cold it is time to begin to wear Spensers and my Nankeen one is very shabby I wish you would send me one and a Bonnet. I hope my Father told you about my Green Frock it is quite rotten. I wish you would send me some stuff for a new one.

from a letter from Betty Bury to her sister Mary,
about 1815

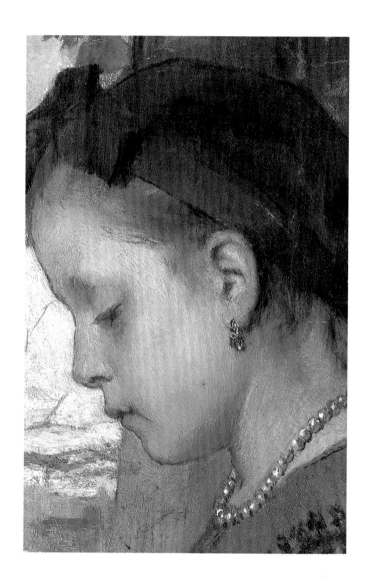

STANISLAS-VICTOR-
EDMOND LÉPINE
(1835–1892) French
*Nuns and Schoolgirls
in the Tuileries Gardens,
Paris*
1871–83

Our dress was of the
coarsest and quaintest
kind, but was respected
out of doors, and is so. It
consisted of a blue
drugget gown, or body,
with ample skirts to it; a
yellow vest underneath in
winter-time; small clothes
of Russia duck; worsted
yellow stockings; a
leathern girdle; and a little
black worsted cap, usually
carried in the hand. I
believe it was the ordinary
dress of children in
humble life during the
reign of the Tudors.

We used to flatter ourselves that it was taken from the monks; and there went a monstrous tradition, that at one period it consisted of blue velvet with silver buttons. It was said, also, that during the blissful era of the blue velvet, we had roast mutton for supper; but that the small-clothes not being then in existence, and the mutton suppers too luxurious, the eatables were given up for the ineffables.

from *Autobiography*,
LEIGH HUNT, 1850

ITALIAN, FLORENTINE
Portrait of a Boy
about 1545

(Lady, to her son)
You have almost atteyned to the age of nyne yeares, at least
to eight and a halfe, and seeing that you knowe your
dutie...Think not that the nobilitie of your ancesters doth
free you to do all that you list, contrarywise, it bindeth you
more to follow vertue...Come hether both of you, doe you
weare your cloathes Gentle-men like?
Where is your hat-band? And where is the cipres of yours?
Have you taken cleane shirts this morning? Your bands be
not cleane.
Why have taken your waste coates? Is it so colde? Button
your dublet, are you not ashamed to be so untrussed? Where
is your Jerkin? for this morning is somewhat colde: and you
also, take your coate, are you ungirt? Boy [*to servant*]... goe
fetch your Masters silver hatched Daggers, you have not
brushed their breeches. Bring the brushes and brush them
before me, Lord God how dustie they are! They are full of
dust, what stockins have you? Your silke stockins or your
worsted hose?

Put on your garters
embroidered with silver,
for it may be that ye shall
goe foorth with me. Where
are your Cuffes
and your falles? Have you
clean handkerchers? Take
your perfumed gloves that
are lyned. Put on your
gownes untill we go and
then you shall take your
cloakes lyned with
Taffata, and your Rapiers
with silver hiltes.

from *Dialogue*,
CLAUDIUS HOLLYBAND, 1568

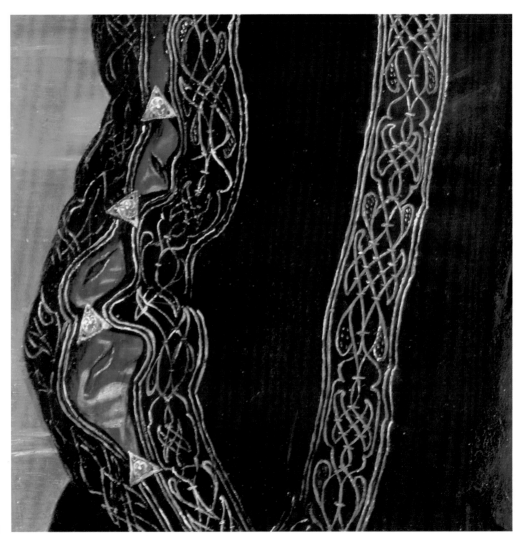

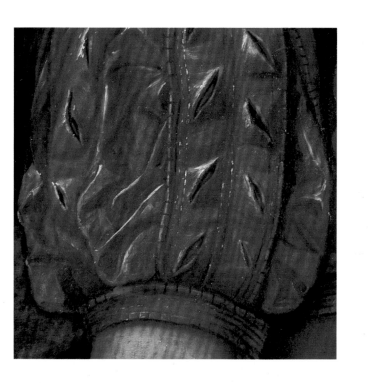

ANTHONY VAN DYCK (1599–1641) Flemish
The Balbi Children
about 1625–27

Joy to Philip, he this day
Has his long coats cast away,
And (the childish season gone)
Puts the manly breeches on.
Officer on gay parade,
Redcoat in his first cockade,
Bridegroom in his wedding trim,
Birthday beau surpassing him,
Never did with conscious gait
Strut about in half the state,
Or the pride (yet free from sin)
Of my little manikin:
Never was there pride, or bliss,
Half so rational as his.
Sashes, frocks, to those that need 'em—
Philip's limbs have got their freedom—
He can run, or he can ride,
And do twenty things beside,
Which his petticoats forbad:
Is he not a happy lad?
Now he's under other banners,
He must leave his former manners;
Bid adieu to female games,
And forget their very names,

Puss-in-corners, hide and seek,
Sports for girls and punies weak!
Baste-the-bear he now may play at,
Leapfrog, football, sport away at,
Show his strength and skill at cricket,
Mark his distance, pitch his wicket,
Run about in winter's snow
Till his cheeks and fingers glow,
Climb a tree, or scale a wall,
Without any fear to fall.
If he get a hurt or bruise,
To complain he must refuse,
Though the anguish and the smart
Go unto his little heart,
He must have his courage ready,
Keep his voice and visage steady,
Brace his eyeballs stiff as drum,
That a tear may never come;
And his grief must only speak
From the colour in his cheek.
This and more must he endure,
Hero in miniature!
This and more must now be done
Now the breeches are put on.

Going into Breeches,
CHARLES & MARY LAMB, late 18th century

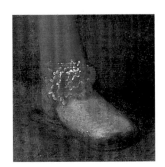

WILLIAM HOGARTH (1697–1764) English
The Graham Children
1742

The first reformation in my appearance was effected by a
stay-maker. I was stood on the window seat whilst a man
measured me for the machine, which in consideration of my
youth, was to be only what was called half-boned, that is
instead of having the bones placed as close as they could lie,
an interval, the breadth of one was left vacant between each.
Notwithstanding, the first day of wearing them was very
nearly purgatory, and I question if I was sufficiently aware
of the advantage of a fine shape to reconcile me to the
punishment.

from *Elizabeth Ham, 1783–1820*,
ELIZABETH HAM, early 19th century

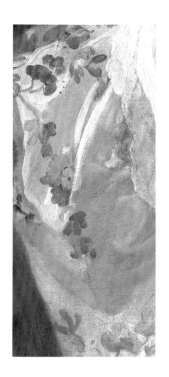

101

GONZALES COQUES
(1614/18–1684)
Flemish
A Family Group
about 1664

*The dress of children
should be different from
that of adults.* – It is
disgusting to behold a
child disfigured by dress,
so as to resemble a
monkey rather than a
human creature…
A suitable dress for young
people ought to shew, by
the contrast it forms to
that of adults, how far the
latter have trespassed
upon the laws of decorum,
and how little attention is
generally paid to health
and convenience.

from *A Familiar View of the
Domestic Education of Children*,
DR CHRISTIAN AUGUSTUS STRUVE,
1802

107

accessories

ATTRIBUTED TO THE
STUDIO OF RUBENS
(Peter Paul Rubens,
1577–1640, Flemish)
*Portrait of the
Infanta Isabella*
before 1615

There is no amendment in
anything that I can see,
neither in one thing nor in
other, but every day worse
and worser, for they not
only continue their great
ruffes still, but also use
them bigger than ever
they did. And whereas
before they were too bad,
now they are past all
shame and honestie, yea
most abhominable and
detestable, and such as
the divell himselfe
would be ashamed to
weare the like.

from *Anatomy of Abuses
in England in 1583,*
PHILIP STUBBES

113

RAPHAEL (1483–1520)
Italian
*Saint John the Baptist
Preaching*
1505

Every article of wear is
extravagantly fashioned
…Hats are of all fantastic
shapes and some people
will have no kind of hat
without a great bunch of
feathers of divers and
sundry colours, peaking
on top of their heads, not
unlike coxcombs…
Men's hats are sharp on
crown, like a church
steeple, standing a
quarter of a yard above
the crown of the head,
or flat and broad on the
crown like the battlements
of a house.

from *Anatomy of Abuses
in England in 1583,*
PHILIP STUBBES

117

ATTRIBUTED TO ROBERT TOURNIERES
(1667–1752) French
La Barre and other Musicians
about 1710

9 May 1663: At Mr Jarvas's my old barber, I did try two or three borders and periwigs, meaning to wear one, and yet I have no stomach for it, but the pains of keeping my hair clean is so great. He trimmed me, and at last I parted, but my mind was almost altered from my first purpose, from the trouble that I foresee will be in wearing them also.

2 November 1663: …without more ado I went up and there he [Mr Jarvas, the barber] cut off my haire, which went a little to my heart at present to part with it, but, it being over, and my periwig on, I paid him £3 for it, and away went he, with my own haire, to make up another of.

from *Diary*,
SAMUEL PEPYS, 1663

123

124

FOLLOWER OF BRONZINO
(Bronzino, 1503–1572, Italian)
Portrait of a Lady
probably 1575–85

Learn now the ways and means, when sleep has left you,
 Of looking bright and fresh and fair of face.
Take barley brought by sea from Libyan farmlands
 And strip away the chaffy carapace.
Then measure out two pounds of your husked barley
 And beat ten eggs with vetch of the same weight.
When airy draughts have dried this, make a donkey
 Grind it on the rough stone with his slow gait.
Grind with it, too, two ounces of the antlers
 First fallen from a stag that long years lives;
And when it's blended with the mealy powder,
 Sift everything at once in fine-meshed sieves.
Add twelve narcissus bulbs—first skin and pound them
 In a clean marble mortar vigorously,
Then gum and Tuscan seed, of each two ounces,
 With honey of nine times that quantity,
A girl who treats her face with that prescription,
 Smoother than her own mirror will appear.

from *Cosmetics for Ladies*,
OVID, 1st century AD

THOMAS DE KEYSER (1596/7–1667) Dutch
Portrait of Constantijn Huygens and his (?) Clerk
1627

Wide bucket-tops are now only seen on heavy boots, the
lighter boots worn today have dropped down to the spurs,
and have only a peak in front and behind. As to the canons
[flounces] displayed above the boots, we like them very large
and of fine starched lawn although they then resemble paper
lanterns. And we like them even more ornate, of two or three
rows of *point de Gènes*, which should be the same for the
jabots. You know that ribbons and points are called *la petite
oye*, and the opening of the shirt in front is called the *jabot*,
and it must always be trimmed with lace, for it is only an old
fogey who buttons his doublet all the way down. Let's go
back to the boots: they must always be long in the foot even
if that is extravagant and against nature…Then the spurs,
they must be of heavy silver, and you must keep changing
their designs without heeding the cost. Those who wear silk
stockings should always have English ones, and the garters
and shoe rosettes should be as fashion dictates.

from *Les Loix de la Galanterie*,
ANONYMOUS, 1644

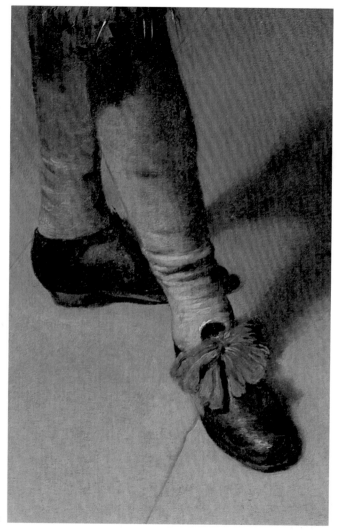

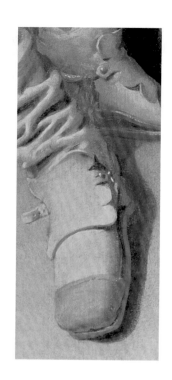

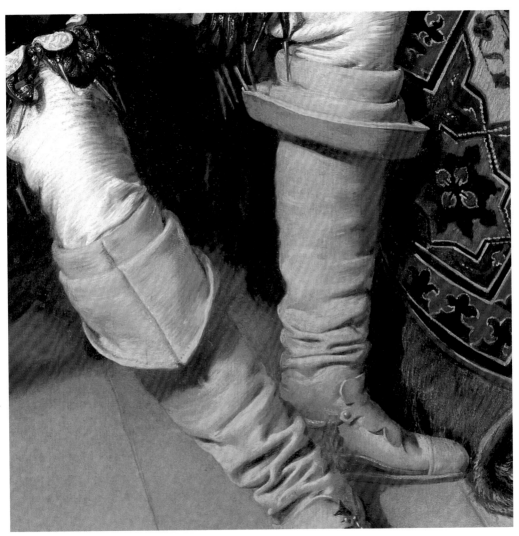

DIEGO VELÁZQUEZ (1599–1660) Spanish
Philip IV of Spain in Brown and Silver
about 1631–32

Sixty pairs of fine silk upper hose
Seven pairs of silk under hose
Three pairs of thread hose
Fifty-six pairs of fine worsted hose
Sixty-nine pairs of white under hose
Forty-four pairs of boothose with welted tops
Four pairs scalloped and laced
Thirty-five pairs of fine tennis hose
Five pairs of tennis silk garters
Forty-eight pairs of tennis socks
Sixty-four pairs of 'foote socks'

list of hose ordered by Charles I,
1633–34

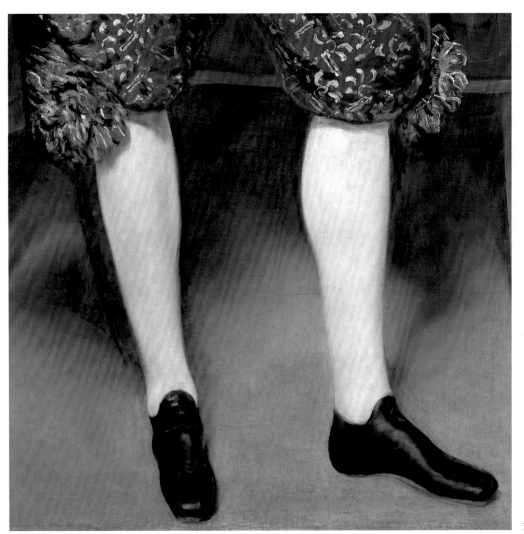

IMITATOR OF
JEAN-BAPTISTE PATER
(Jean-Baptiste Pater,
1695–1736, French)
The Dance
18th century

If the hat is too large in the
crown or too little, the first
will be difficult to keep in
its proper place and the
latter will be equally as bad
to take off. The hat should
always be cocked unless the
weather be bad to prevent
it. Nothing makes a Man
appear more clownish than
a slouched hat, and partic-
ularly in a Dancing School
or in dancing a Minuet.

To have the brim of your hat large and the crown high is awkward; it is always foppish to have your hat too little, that is not to appear larger than a Scotch bonnet or a Jockey's cap (this seems to be the present frothy fashion).

from *The Young Gentleman's and Lady's Polite Tutor*,
M. TOWLE, 1770

ARTISTS & PAINTINGS

BATONI, Pompeo Girolamo
Portrait of a Gentleman
oil on canvas,
134.6 x 96.3 cm, p.69

BORCH, Gerard ter
Portrait of a Young Man
oil on canvas,
67.3 x 54.3 cm, p.55

BRONZINO, Follower of
Portrait of a Lady
oil on wood,
58.7 x 48.6 cm, p.127

CHARDIN, Jean-Siméon
The Cistern (La Fontaine)
oil on canvas,
37.5 x 44.5 cm, p.15

COQUES, Gonzales
A Family Group
oil on canvas,
64.2 x 85.5 cm, p.105

DUYSTER, Willem
*Soldiers Fighting over Booty
in a Barn*
oil on oak,
37.6 x .57 cm, p.59

DYCK, Anthony van
The Balbi Children
oil on canvas,
219 x 151 cm, p.93

*Lady Elizabeth Thimbelby
and Dorothy, Viscountess
Andover*
oil (identified) on canvas,
132.1 x 149 cm, p.19

*Lord John Stuart and his
Brother, Lord Bernard Stuart*
oil (identified) on canvas,
237.5 x 146.1 cm, p.43

EECKHOUT, Gerbrand van den
*Four Officers of the
Amsterdam Coopers' and
Wine-rackers' Guild*
oil on canvas,
163 x 197 cm, p.40

GHIRLANDAIO, Domenico
*A Legend of Saints Justus
and Clement of Volterra*
tempera on wood,
painted surface 14 x 39.4 cm,
p.50

GIOLFINO, Niccolò
Attributed, *The Giusti
Family of Verona (?)*
oil on canvas,
55 x 153 cm, p.110

HOGARTH, William
The Graham Children
oil on canvas,
160.5 x 181 cm, p.98

INGRES, Jean-Auguste-
Dominique
Madame Moitessier
oil on canvas,
120 x 92.1 cm, p.8

Monsieur de Norvins
oil (identified) on canvas,
laid down on panel,
97.2 x 78.7 cm, p.65

ITALIAN, FLORENTINE
Portrait of a Boy
oil on wood,
129 x 61 cm, p.87

KEYSER, Thomas de
*Portrait of Constantijn
Huygens and his (?) Clerk*
oil on oak,
92.4 x 69.3 cm, p.129

LANCRET, Nicolas
The Four Ages of Man:
Childhood
oil on canvas,
33 x 44.5 cm, p.76

LEIGHTON, Baron Frederic
Cimabue's Celebrated
Madonna is carried in
Procession through the Streets
of Florence
oil on canvas,
222 x 521 cm, p.2

LÉPINE, Stanislas-Victor-
Edmond
Nuns and Schoolgirls in the
Tuileries Gardens, Paris
oil on wood,
15.7 x 23.7 cm, p.83

MARIS, Jacob
A Girl Seated Outside a House
oil on mahogany,
32.7 x 20.9 cm, p.79

NEER, Eglon Hendrik van der
Judith
oil on oak,
32 x 24.6 cm, p.11

PATER, Jean-Baptiste
Imitator,
The Dance
oil on canvas,
74.9 x 114.9 cm, p.136

RAPHAEL
Saint John the Baptist
Preaching
egg (identified) on wood,
23 x 53 cm, p.117

RENOIR, Pierre-Auguste
The Umbrellas
oil (identified) on canvas,
180.3 x 114.9 cm, p.29

RUBENS, Peter Paul
Portrait of the Susanna
Lunden (?)
('Le Chapeau de Paille')
oil on oak,
79 x 54.6 cm, cover

RUBENS, Peter Paul
Attributed to the Studio,
Portrait of the Infanta
Isabella
oil on canvas,
120.5 x 88.8 cm, p.113

SUSTERMANS, Justus
Double Portrait of the Grand
Duke Ferdinand II of
Tuscany and his Wife Vittoria
della Rovere
oil on canvas,
161 x 147 cm, p.73

TOURNIERES, Robert
Attributed, *La Barre and*
Other Musicians
oil on canvas,
160 x 127 cm, p.123

VELÁZQUEZ, Diego
Philip IV of Spain in Brown
and Silver
oil on canvas,
195 x 110 cm, p.132

VIGÉE LE BRUN, Elizabeth
Louise
Self Portrait in a Straw Hat
oil (identified) on canvas,
97.8 x 70.5 cm, p.25

ZOFFANY, Johann
Mrs Oswald
oil (identified) on canvas,
226.5 x 158.8 cm, p. 34

WRITERS & WORKS

ANONYMOUS
French
Les Loix de la Galanterie
1644, p.129

English
Monsieur-à-la-mode,
18th century, p.58

BURY, Betty
(b.1800) English
Letter to her sister Mary,
about 1815, p.78

BULWER, John
English
The Artificial Changeling,
1650, p.18

CHAUCER, Geoffrey
(*c.*1343–1400) English
The Canterbury Tales,
from 1387, p.48

CHESTERFIELD, Lord
(1694–1773) English
Letters to his Son,
1745, p.54

DICKENS, Charles
(1812–1870) English
Pickwick Papers,
1836–37, p.72

HAM, Elizabeth
(b. 1783) English
Elizabeth Ham, 1783–1820,
p.99

HAZLITT, William
(1778–1830) English
'On Fashion' from *Sketches
and Essays,* 1839, p.42

HOLLYBAND, Claudius
English
Dialogue, 1568, p.86

HUNT, Leigh
(1784–1859) English
Autobiography, 1850, p.82

LAMB, Charles
(1775–1834) English
Going into Breeches,
late 18th century, p.92

LAMB, Mary
(1764–1847) English
Going into Breeches,
late 18th century, p.92

OVID
(43BC–AD18) Roman
Cosmetics for Ladies,
1st century AD, p.126

PARKER, Dorothy
(1893–1967) American
The Satin Dress, 1926, p.10

PEPYS, Samuel
(1633–1703) English
Diary, 1663, p.122

PUREFOY, Henry
English
*Purefoy Letters –
1735–53,* p.68

RAVERAT, Gwen
(1885–1957) English
*Period Piece, A Cambridge
Childhood,* 1952, p.28

RICHARDSON, Samuel
(1689–1761) English
Pamela; or Virtue Rewarded,
1740–41, p.14

SAUSSURE, César de
French
*A Foreign View of England
in the Reigns of George I &
George II,* 1729, p.35

STANLEY, Lady
English
*The Early Married Life of
Maria Josepha,* 1800, p.64

ACKNOWLEDGMENTS

STRUVE, Dr Christian
Augustus
English
*A Familiar View of the
Domestic Education of
Children,* 1802, p.104

STUBBES, Philip
(active 1583–1591) English
*Anatomy of Abuses in
England in 1583*
p.112 and p.116

TOWLE, M.
English
*The Young Gentleman's and
Lady's Polite Tutor,*
1770, p.137

VIGÉE LE BRUN, Elizabeth
Louise
(1755–1842) French
Souvenirs, about 1835, p.24

The editor and publishers
gratefully acknowledge permission to reprint copyright
material below:

The Satin Dress by Dorothy
Parker, copyright 1926,
renewed 1954 by Dorothy
Parker, from 'The Portable
Dorothy Parker' by Dorothy
Parker, introduction by
Brendan Gill by permission
of Viking Penguin, a division
of Penguin Putnam Inc.

The Satin Dress by Dorothy
Parker from 'Collected
Dorothy Parker' by permis-
sion of Gerald Duckworth &
Co. Ltd.

*Period Piece: A Cambridge
Childhood* by Gwen Raverat
published by Faber & Faber
Ltd by kind permission of the
Faber & Faber Ltd.

Diego Velázquez: detail of *Philip IV of Spain in Brown and Silver*

Title page: Frederic, Baron Leighton of Stretton: *Cimabue's Celebrated Madonna is carried in Procession through the Streets of Florence*, 1853–55

Women's Clothes title page: Jean-Auguste-Dominique Ingres: *Madame Moitessier*, 1856

Men's Clothes title page: Gerbrand van den Eeckhout: *Four Officers of the Amsterdam Coopers' and Wine-rackers' Guild*, 1657

Children's Clothes title page: Nicolas Lancret: *The Four Ages of Man: Childhood*, 1730–35

Accessories title page: Attributed to Niccolò Giolfino: *The Guisti Family of Verona(?)*, probably about 1520